Ina G. Sommermeier

The Correct Seat

Tips for riders on how
to achieve better balance

CADMOS
EQUESTRIAN

Contents

Thoughts Before Mounting

Another book on the correct seat? After all, sitting isn't an art, we do it all the time: in front of the television, at school, in the car, in the office and so on. Each riding style requires a different posture – where does the term "the correct seat" fit in there? The lowest common denominator of all equestrian wisdom is the requirement for the rider to have a relaxed, balanced seat. Once you have acquired this basic skill, you can train and diversify to any equestrian sports discipline you choose. The independent seat is not a rigid shape, not a fixed pattern, but rather depends on the individual conditions of the person riding. And it is recreated anew every second.

The "correct seat" acts and reacts, guides the horse and absorbs its motion – the rider learns to "make an effort" on a physical level, learns to "be in control". That in turn teaches the rider much more than simply "seating himself" correctly.

"Sitting" in everyday life – either with concentration or in a relaxed manner – differs markedly from the posture on a horse.

Horse and Rider Statue – Exercises on the Stationary Horse

Everyone talks about the seat: practising the seat, correction of the seat, exercises for the seat, mounting, sitting deep in the saddle, dressage seat, jumping seat; what is so difficult about sitting on a horse's back that we think about it so much? Didn't we, after all, learn to sit at a very young age? Is it not something we learn in the first a few others. Observe the posture your body adopts: how much does the torso angle towards the thighs, how much weight is carried in each case by the thighs, by the feet?

Exercise "Sitting consciously"

Sit down on as many pieces of furniture as possible: kitchen chair – office furniture – sofa – edge of a bed – car seat – edge of a table – bar stool – gymnastic ball. Maybe you can think of

A sitting position that no one can keep up for long.

years of our lives? And don't we spend most of our waking days sitting down?

Next time you mount a horse, please take a minute before riding off:

Exercise "Horse and Rider Statue I"

Imagine that you are modelling for a large bronze statue of a horse and rider. How do you want to be immortalised for posterity? Place yourself in the right position: straight, balanced, confident, correct. How fast would the artist have to work? You would not be allowed to move, would have to sit completely immobile. How long would you be able to keep that up?

If you agree to this experiment, you are probably hoping that the artist will finish his work

quickly – and that you will be allowed to move again. Now ask somebody to lead your horse forward at a walk and concentrate entirely on the feeling of your seat. Can you feel how much the motion of the horse affects your seat, possibly brings it into disarray? You may have guessed it, and the exercises will have confirmed it: the usual conception of sitting down does not help us at all, when we are sitting on a horse. Preconceptions and physical experiences which can be related to the term "sitting" get us nowhere when it comes to riding. Why? On the muscular level, "sitting" implies a relatively passive posture of the body. (As an aside, long ago, writing for example was not carried out sitting at a desk but instead standing up!) The axis of the body is bent, to a lesser or greater extent, your centre of balance shifts behind the vertical and is supported by the buttocks. As long as the horse stands quietly, we can bend ourselves correctly with a bit of practice, even come quite near to achieving the correct seat, as taught by books on equitation. As soon as the horse begins to move, however, our physical experiences of the body which we connect to the term "sitting" no longer suffice. At that moment the body, in a reflex reaction which is consequently very difficult to control, takes care of its own safety. Our muscles tense up and our arms and legs try to cling – the causes of many faults in our riding seat.

Exercise "Playing ball while sitting down"

Find a number of people who are happy to try an experiment with you. Sit down on stools – and start playing ball. Keep throwing the ball faster and faster and with less regularity. How long will you be able to remain seated?

Kathryn is searching for the feeling of "standing" on the horse – at the moment she would still lose her balance.

Exercise "Horse and Rider Statue II"

Imagine once again that you are modelling for a bronze statue of a horse and rider. This time adopt a comfortable position and imagine that you are standing in the saddle. Try it out: sit down comfortably – follow the idea of standing in the saddle with your posture. Change from "sitting" to "standing" and back a few times. Would you be able to remain immobile as a model for a longer period now? What happens if somebody takes the horse and leads it forward at the walk?

This rider is practising the change of posture from sitting to standing.

You were able to experience it during the exercise: when we react, when we want to move fast, we almost automatically stand up. And this is the key to developing a responsive, active posture on the horse: the concept of standing in the saddle.

Exercise "Standing in the saddle"

Forget for the moment everything you have ever learned about the correct seat. Try out a position on the horse which feels comfortable – and imagine that you are standing. Take up the position in which you would land safely on the ground on both feet and remain standing should the horse suddenly vanish into thin air.

If you like, you can transfer this exercise to the experiment you tried earlier.

Stephanie sitting in the correct seat.

The posture of the rider is generally called "sitting in the saddle". We will continue to use this term. What is important, is to separate the term "sitting" from preconceptions which hinder us when we are riding, and to replace them instead with images which facilitate riding and which address helpful automatic reactions in the body.

Criteria for the Correct Seat

Now compare your seat derived from the concept of standing with the criteria for the correct seat:

• The vertical line: shoulder – hip – heel.
• The buttocks are resting in the deepest point of the saddle, the weight is distributed evenly on both buttocks and the inner thigh muscles.
• The feet are underneath the centre of balance of the rider.
• The feet are resting in the stirrups more or less parallel to the horse's body.
• The heels are the lowest point.
• The spine is upright in its natural S-shape, precisely over the centre of the saddle.
• The head is carried free and upright.
• The shoulders are taken back naturally without force.
• The arms hang down slightly in front of the vertical line and lie gently against the torso.
• The hands are closed as fists without being tightened.
• The lower arm – reins – horse's mouth form a straight line.

The Dynamic Seat – The Feeling of Balance

Now we have to transfer our experiences on the stationary horse into motion. Riding is by its nature an activity of motion, in space and time.

Exercise "How does motion affect the body?"

Once more, sit in the saddle in a relaxed manner. If necessary put your hand inside the front of the pommel or on a small loop attached to the front D-rings of the saddle, the so-called "emergency strap". Try to be as passive as possible. Let somebody lead the horse forwards in an energetic walk. Which forces influence your body? In which directions is your balance upset – and which muscles do you need to use to get back into position?

It is important for the exercises in the following chapters that the horse walks forwards energetically. You, on the other hand, can ride with a loose rein or ask an assistant to lead you or take you on the lunge-rein. This way, you can concentrate on yourself and focus your perceptions inwards. You can create a free space to learn and try things out. The more secure you feel, the more you can go into the game of bracing and relaxing, the deeper you can investigate the secret of balance. Many factors have an effect on the muscles of the body: experiences, intentions, expectations, fears – it is impossible for us to perceive them all consciously. And that is quite all right. Of course, you can perform the exercises without holding on with your hands. By holding on, however, you give your animal the signal that you are looking after yourself well – it can feel safe. As long as you have a hold with your hands, the legs can relax and get the freedom to feel.

The Seat - The Buttocks

The basis of our riding ability is the direct contact between our body and the saddle or the horseback. This is where the weight is concentrated; here we acquire the security which standing on the ground gives us.

Stephanie demonstrates in an exaggerated way which forces the rider is subjected to when the horse starts to walk forwards.

7

You can perform these exercises one after the other or alternating, and you will find that your bearing in the saddle changes. You will sink "deeper into the saddle". If you concentrate on your feeling, you will find that the pressure of the weight of your body is concentrated on two areas: the two ischial tuberosities (commonly known as seat bones). These small bone protuberances are approximately four to five centimetres long and can be found at the lowest point of the osseous pelvic girdle in the form of a slight rocker. As we hardly notice them in our daily life, most of us are unaware they exist – it could be that you will not find them immediately.

The buttocks are pressed together which lifts the body above the saddle. Then the muscles are relaxed and the bottom nestles into the saddle.

The tensed-up muscles of the thigh lift the buttocks out of the saddle; the rider sits deep when they are relaxed.

Exercise "Feeling the saddle"

Initially, concentrate on the pressure which develops between the saddle and your body. Then press the buttocks together firmly, hold them for a moment and relax the muscles once more. If you like, you can assist the relaxation by simultaneously breathing out. Then tense up and relax your muscles a few times. How does this change your contact with the saddle?

Sometimes, this exercise alone has no effect whatsoever, so try the following one as well:

Exercise "Tensing of the Thighs"

Pull your knees up slightly and tense up the muscles of the thighs as tight as possible. Then, as before, relax the muscles and breathe out at the same time. Repeat this exercise two to three times.

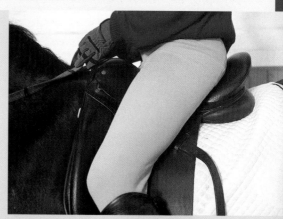

Exercise "Getting to know the seat bones"

Sit on your horse as relaxed as you possibly can (remember, we are standing in the saddle). Let your legs hang down to either side and keep on breathing normally. Now pull in your tummy slightly and relax it again – and pull it back in again, in particular the lower part of your tummy (from below the navel). Now relax it again. When you next pull in the tummy give it a bit of space in the back by making an evasive motion with the spine. Relax again and the spine will follow forwards. During this exercise the muscles of the buttocks remain completely relaxed, and only move far enough not to block the motion backwards and forwards.

As soon as the motion backwards and forwards feels easy to execute, start feeling towards the small rockers, the ischial tuberosities. Gently rock backwards and forwards on them.

This is an exercise which you can also practise on the edge of a chair or table. Primarily make sure that your legs remain relaxed!

You should develop your acquaintance with this part of your body. You will soon realise that you can swing primarily backwards and forwards, but also in all other directions – and the more mobile you are in this area, the easier it will become to go with the motions of the horse. This swinging on the small rockers, balancing on both seat bones, is the key to a relaxed and well-balanced seat.

The mobility of the pelvis, however, is relatively susceptible to interference:

This way you can become acquainted with the ischial tuberosities (ends of the seat bones): if you sit on the front part of the rockers, this eases the weight on the horse's back. Then you move backwards over the centre to the back of the back edges of the rockers which leads to pressure being transferred to the horse's back.

 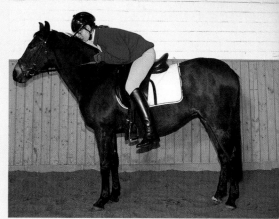

Step 1: First, try out extreme postures.

Exercise "Levering out"

Concentrate on swinging backwards and forwards on the small rockers and

- *press the muscles of the buttocks together – or*
- *hollow your back – or*
- *cling on with your legs – or*
- *squeeze your thighs together.*

What influence do these things have on your mobility?

The Back

We experienced it when we hollowed our back: the posture of our back influences the basis of our mobility. We are taught that we should "sit straight". But what exactly is "straight"? This question is often accompanied by disturbing pictures (often associated with "rigidity", the consequence of which is a hollow back). Therefore, corrections from the outside only help in the short-term, if at all. Try it out for yourself:

Exercise "Upright posture"

Bend your upper body forwards until it almost touches the horse's neck. Then lean back as far as you can (hold on securely for this). Move backwards and forwards between these two positions and decrease the extent of the motion each time. Somewhere in the middle of lying on the horse's neck and lying back as far as you can, you will get a feeling of "straight". But don't be satisfied with that: test out this vertical line, move backwards and forwards just slightly, testing and checking – until you have the feeling that you are completely in balance between the forward and backward position, in balance between the tightening of the muscles of the stomach and those of the back.

Now you will be able to test this feeling for "straight" any time. The more often you practise it, the more easily you will find it again.

This exercise can be expanded any way you wish: each person has their own perception for "straight", "vertical", "in balance", and similar feelings which they can develop to get a more

Step 2: Moving between the extremes ...   *... we find the golden mean.*

objective feel. If you train these perceptions, you will find "your measure" with your posture and will orientate yourself in line with

Exercise "Straight back"

In a similar fashion to the last exercise, now change between hollowing your back and hunching forward in the saddle. Again, reduce the extent of the motion until your back is in balance between the forward and backward positions.

Kathryn demonstrates the extremes of hollowing the back and hunching forwards in the saddle.

your own individual anatomical and physiological conditions. Riders often complain about backaches, especially after a lesson. Backache is caused by excessive tensioning of the muscles. This exercise can help you alleviate and even prevent backache. It can also be used for finding the balance between the right and the left: simply tip over to the right as far as possible – and then to the left – and consequently find the centre position.

Eli balances her head in the vertical. For this purpose she creates an imaginary axis with her index fingers, on which she moves her head.

With its weight of between five and seven kilograms, the head is, potentially, a significant weight aid. If it is drooping forwards, it pulls the mass of the rider towards the forehand of the horse. If it is carried freely, on the other hand, its weight supports the centre of balance and allows the rider to have oversight and farsightedness – in the metaphorical form, concentration and presence.

Exercise "Experience the vertical"
Secure the reins to ensure that they cannot slip down the horse's neck. Then stretch both arms up, place both hands together above your head, create a roof into which you can look comfortably. Hold your arms upwards so that you only have to raise your eyes to look into the hands. (Important: look into the hands, not at the roof of the indoor school or similar – that will soon make you feel dizzy!) Hold this position for a few moments and then release your arms with smooth circles of both arms. You can go back immediately to that position, build a roof – and then let the arms circle. Pay attention to how large you become in the saddle – without having to change your posture significantly!

This exercise helps you experience the vertical.

As we are currently in the process of ascertaining the balance to find the centre, we should also concentrate on the other end of the spine, the head. This is a part of the body you can also experiment with – backwards and forwards – to ascertain in which position the head becomes the "dot over the i" of the longitudinal axis. How high do you carry the nose – the chin – your line of vision? Search for your own measure again, find your inner balance.

The Seat – The Legs

In addition to the seat bones, our weight rests evenly on the insides of the thighs – at least if these are prepared to carry the weight. If, on the other hand, you involuntarily cling to the horse, you block the mobility of the pelvis and push yourself out of the saddle instead of keeping yourself deep and secure. This reflex can only be overcome with patience. The more we are used to the processes of motion on horseback, the easier we will find it to relax our legs.

One immediate measure is using the hands to find a secure hold. Another measure is to eliminate the effect of the clinging muscles by carefully turning the legs, along their entire length, inward from the hip. In most people, the muscles of the torso are shortened due to faulty posture, which means that this motion initially causes us to hollow our back.

Warning

■ ■ ■ ■

"Turning the legs inward versus hollowed back" Please make sure that your back stays mobile and that the seat bones remain clearly tangible! To begin with; turn the legs inwards only slightly. Then correct the position, loosen up with a bit of gymnastics – and in time work your way into the necessary extension.

The ischial tuberosities, the vertical, the head, the legs, and the posture from head to toe should remain nicely locked at all times. In order to ensure that you continue to enjoy yourself with everything which needs to be taken into consideration, we now have an exercise which is a reminder that our main aim of sitting in the saddle is to have fun:

Exercise "Caricatures"

Forget for one moment everything which you know – and simply enjoy sitting on your horse and being carried by it. Then pull up your knees and heels appreciatively, sit on the horse as you should never do otherwise. Your head? Let it drop forward. And as to hollowing your back? How do cartoon riders jump over fences? Copy them! Or sit down in the saddle with the pretentious affectation of the know-all. Or pretend to be scared.

Exaggerate in every way (similarities to any living persons are purely coincidental!). Let your imagination run free, try out everything you can think of.

Afterwards, you can relax and be yourself again – how do you feel now?

Caricatures – let us not forget: riding is fun!

Communicating With the Horse's Back – The Feeling for Motion

The Walk

Having occupied ourselves with the physical conditions, felt inside ourselves and experimented with positions, we will now turn to the contact with the horse's back and consider the exchange of dialogue between horse and rider.

Exercise "What happens underneath the saddle?"

Let your horse walk a few rounds in the school on a loose rein, relax in the saddle – and this time forget everything you have learned about the order of the leg movement.

- *What do you feel underneath the saddle?*
- *How would you describe this to a child?*
- *Is there an image for it?*
- *Are there differences between right and left?*

Some riders describe the motion as a "wave" which rolls from left to right and back, others use the image of a bicycle or of a hill and a valley. Everyone has his or her personal image. I will use the term "wave", but you can exchange your own term for it.

Exercise "Playing with the horse's back"

The next thing to do is to play with the motion which is coming up from below. Try making way for the incoming wave, once on the right, once on the left. Let your hips turn small circles, first in the one direction, then in the other.

The instruction to sit "deeper into the saddle" does not mean to plump down on it and to keep both buttocks as firmly secured to the saddle as possible. If you do this, you will find that the pelvis becomes tense, the legs tense up – and any feeling for the horse's back motion disappears. You will find the secret of the "deep seat" as soon as you give in to the rhythm of the motion of the horse.

How do we manage to make our pelvis mobile enough that it swings in tune with the horse's back? Joni Bentley offers a good model for this ability:

Exercise "Riding with duck's feet"

Imagine that your two ischial tuberosities are not simply two small rockers but broad duck's feet which are sitting squarely on the right and left side of the saddle. Try to dance with these on the horse's back.

If you wish, we can take this image one step further.

Exercise "Duck's feet in rhythm"

Imagine that you are pushing the pedals of a bicycle forwards with your duck's feet, keeping to the rhythm of the horse's back. Which conception best matches the motion from below: pedalling forwards or backwards?

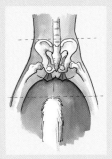
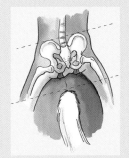
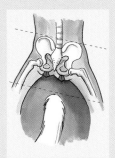

Imagine that you are riding with duck's feet.

Exercise "Horse's back and duck's feet in dialogue"

Once you have adopted the rhythm of the horse's back, gently start consciously to pedal more slowly – only a split second slower that the rhythm of the horse's back – and then another split second slower. Do you receive an answer from the horse? Does it change its tempo?

During these exercises we have paid no attention to our legs. It is now high time to do so:

Stephanie is overdoing it for the photographer – her horse reacts with some irritation. You can see clearly how the rider's leg falls against the horse's side when the horse's rear leg on the same side moves forward.

Exercise "What happens with the legs?"

Be sure to feel exactly what is happening: how are your legs reacting while you are "pedalling your bicycle with the duck's feet"? Do they simply hang down? Does their position change? How is the contact of the rider's legs to the horse's sides?

Once you have attained a feeling for the rhythm, you will find this repeated in the legs: you simply have to feel intensively, and not be thrown by trying to analyse the order of the motion of the horse's legs. To be precise: every time one duck's foot gives way upward, the other duck's foot sinks down – and the attached rider's leg is pulled very slightly against the side of the horse: once on the right, once on the left. Books on equitation describe this as "alternating application of the leg aids". To me, the image of the "rider's leg breathing in and out with the horse" is more expressive.

Exercise "The rider's legs breathing in and out with the horse"

For the purpose of relaxation, we now have an exercise on the ground. Dismount from your horse, let the stirrups hang down and ask somebody to lead the horse away from you in a straight line. Remain standing behind the horse: observe how the stirrups knock against the horse's side with each step. This corresponds exactly to the dynamic of your legs.

If you manage to feel your legs swinging into the horse's side in the same way that you have just observed from the ground, you are on the way to achieving a relaxed seat. This, by the way, is the meaning of the saying that "the horse itself collects its aids to ride forwards". Did you see that the stirrup swings into the side of the horse at the exact moment when the hind leg of the horse on the same side is lifted?

And as we are currently communicating with the horse's back: observe the ears of your horse while your legs are breathing in and out with the horse's motion. To make it even more clear, press gently against the horse's side with the respective leg which is swinging in towards the horse. Exactly! The horse will move its ear on the same side towards you. Sometimes the horse only twitches the tip of the ear, as if it did not hear you correctly. Sometimes – in particular when everything is running smoothly and conformably – you can observe how the horse tries to ignore the impulse. In this case, you are allowed to push a bit harder! And that is an impressive picture. We are able to "talk" with the horse via the body – and somebody is even listening!

So far, we have carried out our exercises only at the walk – and had time to feel the motion and think about it. Before we transfer our experiences to the trot and canter, we should take a short break and, in view of its need for analysing, give the brain some food for thought.

The following is true for the communication between horse and rider: the aid that drives the horse forward only reaches the horse if it is in the process of lifting its hindleg from the ground. How does the rider, however, know when this is happening? From the exercises practised so far we have received precious tips: when a horse places its hindleg on the ground a muscle wave is created which runs out once the horse lifts that leg again. This is precisely the moment in which the rider's leg is pulled against the side of the horse. The small amount of pressure which is created through the contact (or which is increased purposefully) gives the leg that is being lifted the necessary impulse to propel itself forward.

Correlations such as these, form the basis for the dialogue of motion between the rider and the horse, which needs to become ever more fine-tuned.

The Trot

As the image of "standing in the saddle" on the stationary horse helped us attain an appropriate posture, it would seem consistent to compare the seat in motion with images of motion as well – walking, running and hopping. In fact, there are indeed great similarities between riding and walking, i.e. moving forwards without a horse. You will rediscover the motion of the horse's back which we know from the walk at the trot. However, the horse's back is now pushing, indeed "shoving" the rider from below – and that means a great deal of jolting. Security and looseness will have to be conquered anew.

Acting on the conception of "standing up and sitting down", the movements of the rider become excessive and she falls behind the motion of the horse.

In principle, all exercises which you have learned at the walk help. First, however, you will have to relieve the spine: hold on to the saddle and release your spine and then see whether you can find the joint rhythm with the horse's back. Allow the motion of the horse to throw you about a bit and try to dance on the horse's back with the "duck's feet": right – left – right – left. In comparison with the walk, the "dancing steps" at the trot have become very small.

The Rising Trot
However, before your back becomes completely tensed up, use the rising trot to help you. At the rising trot you move with the horse's

back: not to the left and to the right, but instead up and down. The upward motion often becomes excessive and the rider will increasingly fall behind the motion of the horse – and thereby lose the dialogue with the horse. Therefore, we have a further exercise:

Exercise "The rising trot in dialogue"
The best thing is to forget the concept of "standing up" and "sitting down". Concentrate the motion on the area of your pelvis and attempt to stay close to the saddle. And then you need to change the passive being thrown about into an active motion: try using the concept of thinking of the movement downwards when you are rising, anticipate the movement upwards when you are coming down.

Acting on the concept of "easing and putting back your weight", the rider remains in rhythm with the motion and in contact with her horse.

Oh, and by the way, when you are rising to the trot you should always place your feet in the stirrups, otherwise the exercise turns into a strong-man act. With regard to the exercises I have offered you so far, it is a question of taste whether you prefer to ride with or without stirrups. On the one hand, the stirrups give the rider a hold and thereby the feeling of security. On the other hand, there is the danger of the rider tending to stand in the stirrups and holding on by the legs. Unless the legs are relaxed, even well-fitted stirrups become too long, the rider's feet will begin to try to keep them in place, and the rider thereby loses the contact with the seat bones.

On the other hand, the role of the stirrups should not be overestimated: they offer the rider's foot a slight support. The contact of the rider's knees and calves with the horse's sides or the saddle flap give the rider his actual hold. At the rising trot, the upper body can be bent forward slightly – and until the time the rider masters this seat safely, he is allowed to support himself with his hands on the horse's neck.

By the way, you will find it easier to find your balance if you look up at the path you are following. Some riders control the motion of the trot by staring at the horse's shoulder. They have learned to "stand up when the outer shoulder swings forward." This statement is not incorrect, but it is extremely hindering. It increases our tendency to control our motion and hold on with the eyes, and only trust what we can see. This, however, means we are distancing ourselves from our feeling of the body and, thereby, lose the contact with the hindlegs of the horse. "Ride your horse forwards and ride it straight": this famous saying of Gustav Steinbrecht can only be achieved if you are in contact with the hindlegs of the

horse. The following is an exercise which will help you activate your "somataesthesia" (feeling for the body), and teach you to take up this contact:

Exercise
"Rising trot on the hindleg"

Ask somebody to take your horse on the lunge-rein and hold onto the saddle with your hands. If you can, close your eyes. Otherwise determine points of fixation (lamps, posts, trees) on which to move with your eyes while circling. "Correct" and "incorrect" no longer have any meaning, the only thing that counts from now on is the joint motion with the horse – and how your body feels during that time.

The person on the lunge-rein asks your horse to trot. Rise to the trot. After a few strides, change the leg in the trot. What is different now? Balance out the feeling in your body with that of the trot on the other leg. After a further few strides, change the leg again. Does it feel the same as during the first strides? Is it different?

Then change legs again. Which motion is easier to balance, the first or the second?

Now change legs a bit faster, after three or four strides each time. Try to summarise the feeling in your body, for example: "What feels easier?" Play with your weight. Which influence is exerted on the body on the "easier" leg at the rising trot, if you transfer your weight inward to the centre of the lungeing circle – and what, if you transfer your weight to the outside? And only now, after you have become familiarised with your perceptions, try to ask your body to tell you when the inner hindleg swings forward.

This exercise should be carried out on the right and on the left rein. Thus, you will develop a measure for the correct motion and will soon no longer have to listen to the riding school instructor call out: "Wrong leg!"

The next exercise for the rising trot has great merits in those cases where
- unbalanced movements have appeared (for example, standing up too high at the trot, sitting down too heavily)
- a very mechanical up and down can no longer find the rhythm of the horse's back
- the rider feels unable to control his horse at the rising trot as well as he used to
- sometimes some horses find it difficult to loosen up at the rising trot

You can try out the exercise on the lunge-rein, when you are riding independently and out on every hack:

Exercise "Interruption of the pattern"

Normally, you stand up and sit down at the rising trot at a ratio of one to one. Now play around with this rhythm, stay seated for one stride, stand up for two, then change this around: sit out two strides stand up for one. It becomes more difficult when you sit for three strides or stand for two – or even two to five or four to three. Try out every combination you can think of!

This exercise will help you eliminate patterns of motion which have become routine, improve your seat at the rising trot, exercise the contact of your knees and calves with the side of the horse, and make you concentrate – this makes it easier to let go. To begin with the horse will react with surprise, then it will feel relief and willingly enter into the "play", and will in fact offer its back for training.

The Sitting Trot
You can develop the sitting trot in the same playful manner:

Exercise "Learn to sit at the trot"
Starting from the rising trot, stay down for two or three strides, then continue to rise to the trot, sit down again – but only as long as you can remain relaxed. Change back to the rising trot before reflexes to hold on develop, before you tense up your back, before you start feeling pain. Always ensure that your back remains flexible, that your legs are supple. Hold on with your hands. The next time you remain seated, think of the "duck's feet" and dance with them on the "waves" of the horse's back. Let yourself be thrown for two or three strides, search for the rhythm, then rise to the trot again. Keep being nice to the horse and yourself!

Ah yes, the "supple legs" – on the one hand they should remain relaxed, should "breathe" with the horse, on the other hand they are supposed to ensure secure hold and apply pressure every now and then. This is only possible if we are clear in our own mind that we use different muscles for different tasks: tense individual groups of muscles and relax others – in contrast to the "clinging leg", where the flexor muscles are those primarily tensed up and used for holding on. Instead of a lesson in anatomy, I offer you an exercise instead:

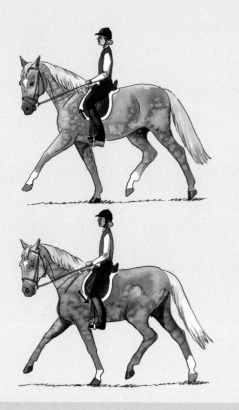

By tensing knees and thighs alternately on each side, the rider manages to "run along at the trot".

The Canter

The canter allows the horse to go at maximum speed, the rider sees images of freedom, of stubble fields, of pirouettes and flying changes, but also of bolting horses. Essentially, the canter is a "type of jumping", as one jump follows the other. The rider will also need to replace his "standing" and "running" with the image of "hopping".

The feeling under the saddle is of a single large wheel rolling on one side (again, find your own image for the motion and use it accordingly). If you feel this large motion on the right side, you are cantering on the right leg. Move your weight slightly to the right and you will experience the motion even more clearly. If the wheel seems to be rolling on the left side, you are cantering on the left leg and should transfer your weight slightly to the left.

Exercise
"The supple leg"

Start trotting at the rising trot, then sit down, remember your flexible back and start to "run" with both legs in tempo with the horse's back. Actively tense the knee and thigh as soon as the horse's back moves up beneath it: right – left – right – left. If you want to keep the tempo, the movements have to become small and rapid. As soon as you have found the rhythm and your balance, make the movements of running smaller, let the motion of the legs become increasingly smooth, until you cannot detect any movement from the outside. Finally only think of the impulse of running along!

Exercise "Sitting at the canter"

Once more let somebody take your horse on the lunge rein. Again, hold on with your hands, but this time in a different way: the outer hand holds the pommel of the saddle, the inner hand is placed on the cantle. Can you still feel your ischial tuberosities, the "duck's feet"? If not, push the inner hip slightly forward so that you are sitting in the saddle with a slight twist. This posture will bring you in line with the posture of the horse and helps to stay with the motion. Now the person holding the lunge-rein asks your horse to canter. Concentrate solely on the rolling movement under the saddle. Make sure that your back remains flexible, and dance on the

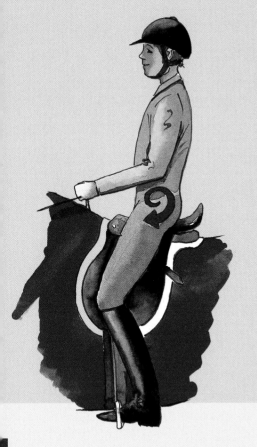

At the canter, the rider follows the horse's back by letting his hips circle with the swinging motion of the horse.

And while we have learned to recognise the motion with the buttocks, we ask ourselves once again: "What happens with the legs?"

Exercise
"Rider's legs at the canter"

Repeat the last exercise and now observe your legs. How are they being moved? Let the inside leg follow the motion along its entire length. Again, this outer movement is one that you will reduce more and more and in the end only send the mental impulse to the muscles. The supple leg will be pulled against the horse's side when the motion of the "wheel" reaches its lowest point. Observe the outside leg: if you don't force it to cling and let it move naturally, it will move against the horse's side on its own and there have the effect of a boundary.

In order to complete this series of exercises and strengthen your feeling for the motion at the canter, we have a further exercise. This is one that you can carry out anywhere, on the lunge-rein, while riding independently in the school or out on a hack.

motion with the "duck's feet" Also experiment by transferring your weight to the outside, moving your upper body forwards or backwards, to the right and to the left, out of line with the motion. What happens with your legs and arms, when you do this? How much power do you need to hold on?

Exercise "Communicating with the horse's back at the canter"

Sitting on the cantering horse, observe your flexible back, the pelvis which is following the circular motion on one side, the leg working in co-ordination with this, and then carefully and slowly start to slow down your movements. It may be that the leg will have to bear a little more pressure on the horse's side (but only a little more). Can you circle even more slowly? And does the horse's back follow your motion? Now circle slightly faster – how does the horse react?

Light Aids – Using the Seat

I would like to introduce the subject of "using the aids" with a typical example from my experience.

A rider asks for a lesson because her horse is difficult to ride forwards. It has been checked over by a vet and is completely healthy. Fitting a new saddle did not bring any improvement either. The rider has spent many hours on the lunge-rein practising seat exercises. Now she is riding her horse on a loose rein – slightly tense in the strange surroundings, but overall looking pleasing. As soon as I ask her to take up the reins, the picture changes dramatically. It can be summarised in the words: "The pleasant relaxation is over – now it's time to start working."

This rider needs to learn that "sitting correctly" is not a question of either–or, not a separate subject as such, but rather the question of the right relationship between relaxation, listening, reacting and feeling, on the one hand, and tensioning, the use of information from the motion, placing of impulses and guidance on the other. In her first lesson she has to learn to let her pelvis move freely. She needs to learn to sit in such a way that her seat becomes a driving aid for her horse.

The wave motion under the saddle is, after all, nothing other than the back muscles of the horse which tighten alternatively on the right and on the left side. If the rider sits immobile, her weight works against the muscles and it becomes difficult for the horse to move its legs. If the rider, on the other hand, moves her pelvis, she will give the muscle space to move, and becomes a lighter burden for her horse. Together with the leg which is breathing with the horse, the forward movement of the horse – once it has started – will be maintained automatically. Thus, the seat of the rider becomes an aid for the horse. In the following exercises, you will receive tips on how to "use yourself correctly", and how to work out a relationship between the seat and influencing the horse with it.

The Weight Aids

One thing is certain: the weight of the rider does not change significantly in the space of an hour: that is, it is impossible to "make yourself heavy" or "make yourself light". However, it is possible to make it more difficult (i.e. heavier) or easier (i.e. lighter) for the horse. And it is possible to distribute your weight differently over the surface of your seat.

The following principle always applies: when riding dressage, the rider ensures through the distribution of his weight that he always maintains his position and the feeling for his vertical posture.

Warning

"Involuntary displacement of the weight" Always stay "with yourself", in the centre of your balance, when transferring your weight! You have to avoid

- leaning into the curve
- bending in the hip
- tilting the upper body sideways
- hanging on to one side of the saddle or to trying to balance yourself on one side.

The most common weight distribution errors. Eli is bending into the curve and Anna is demonstrating the incorrect bending in the hip.

Eckart Meyners suggests that the rider imagines the face of a clock drawn on his seat and that he controls the weight like a hand of the clock: backwards to the "6", forwards to the "12", to the right to the "3" and to the left to the "9". Please also remember when using this image that the seat bones are spaced apart about 10 centimetres and are four to five centimetres long. Thus, the basis for the circular movement is very small and changes occur in the range of a few centimetres.

Apart from the fact that the faulty distribution of the weight always looks a bit funny and makes the rider lose his balance (he will then have to hold on), the horse will be given undesirable, in part contradictory, impulses. The following exercise is suited to the gymnastic ball as well as to the saddle:

Exercise "Weight transfer"

Place both your hands underneath your buttocks and test whether your weight is evenly distributed on both sides. Them move the upper body as best you can, bend in the hip, lean over to one side, lean into an imaginary curve, slip to one side. How does the pressure on your hands change? Can you feel both seat bones at the same time? Does the weight move to the other side under certain circumstances?

Dominique Barbier uses the image of a small dog which balances on a ball with his four paws to illustrate the correct weight transfer (the four paws can be compared to the front and rear ends of the seat bone rockers).

Whatever image you prefer, you will have to remember that the pressure which you are relieving on one side will place an equivalent burden on the other side. Sitting in the motion means moving the pelvis in such a way that you always relieve the muscle of the horse's back which is being tensed (crest of the wave). At the same time your pelvis tilts in the other direction (into the trough of the wave) and there leads to an increased bur-

den. Nowadays, it is difficult to convey the correct movement of the pelvis, as the muscles of the stomach have lost their meaning in our modern life – and how are you expected to tense muscles which you don't know exist or where?

How do you stand when you are waiting in the queue at the cash-out? Do you stand with your weight distributed equally on both legs – or are you relieving one leg? That's where you need the muscles of the stomach.

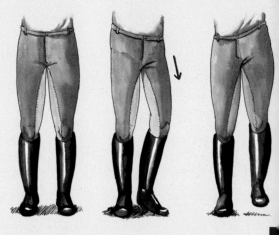

A good exercise for the mobility of the pelvis is to tilt the pelvis to one side and then actively lift it up again.

Exercise "Unilateral weight transfer"

Use the next queue you're standing in. Support yourself on the shopping trolley, for example, place the legs apart about the width of your shoulders, and distribute your weight evenly. Now bend one knee slightly and straighten it again. While doing this, observe the motion with which your pelvis reacts. This gives you an idea as to of which muscles we are talking about. Then change the movement over. Now the pelvis is not dropped over the knee but instead lifted with the stomach muscles. Naturally, you should repeat the exercise with the other leg!

Once the movement is easy and automatic you can start to expand it. Now you stand without a support and lift the pelvis, not only sideways but slanting upwards and forwards. Let go and place the hanging leg back on the ground. Repeat this movement a number of times, then use the other leg. Be satisfied if you achieve a movement of one centimetre! It is better to carry out one small correct movement than a large one which is carried out primarily by the assisting muscles (back, buttocks, legs).

When you are back in the saddle, remind yourself of the muscles which you have become acquainted with in this way. Now use them, either directly or via the image of "riding a bicycle with duck's feet". With this experience of your body also test the image of the clock face and now move the centre of your balance with the help of the stomach muscles.

When you are riding circles, turns, or at the canter, it is not enough to simply relieve and put pressure on each side alternatively. In this case your weight has to be used increasingly via one seat bone alone. For this purpose, you also retain your basic position in the saddle. To use a slight weight aid simply turn your head in the direction in which you wish to ride. As the bend gets sharper you increase the aid by moving your entire upper body into this direction. The outer shoulder moves forward slightly, whereas the inner shoulder moves back. Now observe your seat bones! At a certain point you will probably "lose" one seat bone. You will find it again by taking

When you turn off correctly, the direction of your eyes indicates the new direction and your body adopts a slight turn of the seat.

The weight swings backwards, the upper body remains straight.

the inside hip a fraction forward. Adjusting your seat in this way helps you retain your position without moving about, sliding, or tilting.

We introduced the bilateral weight aid earlier, in the chapter "The Dynamic Seat – The Feeling of Balance". Now, do not pull your pelvis aslant alternately with the straight stomach muscles, but instead forward and upward simultaneously, and at the same time be aware of the rear end of the seat bones. (Remember: they are no longer than four to five centimetres overall!) This constitutes the bilateral weight aid.

The Leg Aids

The position of the legs will sort itself out on its own from the balanced seat, using the inner image of "standing in the saddle". The legs hang down from the hips freely, the calves partially touching the saddle. The relation between the upper and the lower leg depends on the conformation of the rider and that of the horse.

An important aid – although not specifically mentioned – is the bilateral resting of the legs against the horse's side. It forms a framework for the communication between the horse and rider. The consistent smooth contact of the legs demonstrates to the horse whether the rider is expressing an intention or simply trying to keep in balance.

The rider's legs frame the horse.

In order to bring the heel to the horse's side the knee has to be pulled up and the lower leg twisted at an unnatural angle. This disturbs the flow of motion of the horse and rider.

In order to clarify this, a further exercise can be used:

Exercise "Exploring the calf"

The next time you are watching television, for example, sit down comfortably on the sofa, floor, or chair and examine your lower leg with your hands from the knee downward. Where exactly do you feel hard, firm, and soft structures? Which are bones, tendons, muscles? Circle your foot slowly and keep a hand on your calf. Where and how does the muscle change with the movement, where is the muscle mass situated, and where does it move to when the muscle is tightened? Which movement do you need to perform to cause the calf muscle to stand out – similar to the biceps muscle on the arm? And: can you do this without any visibly perceptible movements?

Exercise "The legs frame the horse"

Repeat the exercises from the chapter "Communicating With the Horse's Back – The Feeling for Motion" and test how the horse reacts, when
• the rider's legs are applied gently against both sides of the horse
• the legs are pushed away from the horse's sides.
These include primarily the legs of the rider which are breathing in and out with the motion of the horse. When we ask the horse to walk off, when we ask for full and half-halts, and for more emphatic communications with the horse, we will require a bit more pressure with the legs. And every rider knows: "The leg aids are given with the calves."

If they try out this exercise, riders are always astonished how high up the muscle mass begins and how far the muscle stands out to the side (instead of to the back). As a rule it can be applied

Warning

"Disruptive forward driving aid"
When you look closely, the calf of the rider sometimes seems to consist of the heel and its extension, the spur. However, since neither touch the horse's side when the leg hangs down

naturally, the rider needs to pull up his knee or pull the lower leg back to use the heel on the horse's side. Using a leg aid in this position will come a moment too late at its best and disrupts the flow of motion. It takes the horse by surprise and interrupts its rhythm.

The driving leg lies on the girth, roughly under the rider's centre of gravity.
The restricting leg lies about a hand's width behind the girth.

pressure of the calf shows the horse the direction sideways, which is then immediately restrained by the restricting leg and transferred to the movement forwards. The horse places its feet diagonally forwards and sideways, and crosses over the other pair of legs.

The Mental Aids

to its optimum and with the least effort in the position it is in when the rider is sitting in the balanced "standing seat".

If one calf now presses against the horse's side as a driving impulse, the horse will initially not bend itself around this leg but rather try to move away from it to the other side: high time to use the restricting outside leg. If the rider is riding within a contained area (for example, within the side boards of the indoor school or fence of the outdoor school, or a row of trees along the bridle path), the horse will be unable to move away. The more advanced the rider becomes the more will his restricting lower leg take over the task of controlling the hindquarters. It moves back by about a hand's width, becomes the restricting leg in the fashion of a mobile side fence and specifies the outer frame for the movement.

Neither is the leg that drives the horse forwards diagonally an isolated action. Its function only becomes fully fulfilled in close co-ordination with the restricting leg. In contrast to the forwards driving leg it is moved back slightly. In this position, the

We are now able to direct our horse in any direction we choose by using our weight and legs. In order to reinforce our trust in this ability, we have to learn to impose our control – in the original meaning of the word. It is simply not enough to think: " Well, let's see what happens" and turn our head. Or to introduce the sideways turning seat aid and to ponder whether the horse is going to follow or not, or what to do, if it doesn't: the signals which the horse receives in this case will be timid and contradictory. And to be on the safe side, it will simply not react at all.

"Imposing control" does not mean a more or less rough aid but instead opens up the entire chapter of the mental aids, which is not officially recognised by the traditional equestrian school of thought. Imposing one's control means that the rider is in complete co-ordination with his intentions. He pictures an image, for example that of the bend which he intends to ride, fills his entire being with this image, becomes the bend and mirrors this image with his mobile, balanced body. He wants this bend.

If you want to practise this, it is important to eliminate everything which could be disruptive. Be easy on yourself and your horse. Make up your mind to turn off into the bend, irrespective of where it will finally happen. To begin with, the important thing is that it happens at all.

Exercise
"School figures without reins"

To begin with, secure the reins to ensure that they do not slip down the horse's neck and over its head. If you want to keep the reins in the hands take them by the buckle and then hold onto the "emergency strap" or the inside of the pommel with that hand.

To begin with you should practise simple turns. Turning in by a mere two to three steps from the track counts as a success! The circle is also a suitable track figure for practising . The more secure you become, the more independent your figures will become. You will be able to ride small circles and squiggles anywhere in the school, serpentines, track-independent straight lines, staying on the second or third track. With time the figure you are riding will become more and more similar to the shape you imagined. Always immediately practise every figure you have ridden on one rein on the other rein. Practise introducing and performing the transition from one rein to the other until it becomes increasingly flowing and planned well in advance.

Attention: while you are concentrating on your own riding, do not lose sight of the other riders, as you will soon otherwise become a menace!

You can use this exercise for the time in which the horse is meant to be walked around without being expected to make any particular efforts: time which is sometimes shortened or ignored as wasted time. You can also playfully conclude the work period with this exercise. Those times, during which the riders often dismount, can thus be converted to precious encounters, intensifying the contact to your horse.

The Rein Aids

Oh yes, we almost forgot – now we have to ask ourselves: if we do not have to hold on when we are riding and the horse can also be ridden in any chosen direction without reins – whatever do we need them for? It makes sense not to use the reins until one is able to use them in the sense of light aids. In real life, this is almost impossible to do, but the rider should nevertheless be conscious of what it is he is holding in his hands, and should strive to improve his balance and independent seat. If the rider is well balanced at the walk, trot and canter, his pelvis absorbs the motion of the horse's back and his hands are free to engage in communication with the horse's mouth. The rider's hand is meant to absorb each chewing motion of the horse on the bit, each nodding of the head, each change caused by position and bend. To a large extent, this is very sensitive work, primarily a slight squeezing and easing of

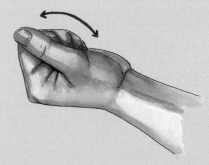

The hands open and close as if squeezing out a face flannel.

hands. These small movements are all but invisible to an observer. The hands remain upright and form a straight line, reaching from the horse's mouth to the elbows. The reins are passed without any twists between the ring finger and small finger through the closed hand. The thumbs form a roof over the reins and hold them firm.

Picture yourself holding a small bird in each hand, which cannot escape but which must not be crushed, to help you imagine how the reins should be held.

The elbows belong to the rider.

The hands of the rider seen from the side and from the viewpoint of the rider.

the hands, as if you were squeezing out a face flannel. Sometimes the entire hand has to be turned inward or outward. If a rein becomes too long because its has slipped through the hand, it will need to be shortened – not corrected by moving back the elbow or the shoulder!

The elbows hang down with the upper arms on both sides from the shoulders and remain close to the rider's side: they belong to the rider – and not to the horse!

Take up the reins as close as you need to feel the contact to the horse's mouth and follow its small movements. Play with the tension in the

Warning

"The elbows belong to the rider"
Every now and then you will see a rider with his arms stretched forward, with the elbows pushed out almost straight. The rider is endangering his balance and secure hold. As soon as the horse jerks its nose forwards or pushes it down, the rider is pulled forward without mercy.

Exercise
"The other end of the reins"

Ask somebody to hold one end of a rein, a lunge-rein or thin rope with his hand. You yourself should take hold of the other end, approximately one metre away from your assistant. One of you begins. By opening and closing the fingertips, either of you specifies the movement of the rein, yielding and tightening, which the other person answers by a responding light opening and closing of their hand. The rein between you and your assistant should remain evenly tensioned; it must not jump, jolt, or be jerked. Change over positions. Try out a silent communication between the hands. One person guides, the other follows, then the second person takes over the guidance the first person follows, and so forth. Always also practise this exercise with the other hand and, eventually, with both hands.

Nevertheless, experience teaches us that the rein aid can be as well prepared as possible, that the well-balanced seat is relatively firmly established – but everything falls apart as soon as the rider picks up the reins. This is due to the fact that in our daily life we are accustomed to direct, hold onto, "have under control" everything with our hands and under supervision of the eyes. We hardly ever use our entire body for any action and don't trust ourselves in this relation.

Exercise "Looking with the back"

Move around in a room with a few friends – keeping your eyes closed. Can you feel if somebody is approaching you? Do you realise it before you bump into somebody? When is the other person approaching? From which direction is he coming, in which direction is he moving?

These exercises are merely suggestions. You can expand them any way you wish. Try, for example, to imagine what is happening in a waiting queue behind you. There is one great exercise for this purpose on the back of a horse which I don't want to keep to myself:

Exercise "Lungeing backwards"

Ask somebody to take your horse on the lunge-rein, fit a vaulting girth on the horse (or a similar suitable surcingle) – and sit backwards on your horse facing its tail. Observe the actions of the croup, the muscle waves flowing through the back. Occasionally close your eyes and draw in the motion deep within yourself.

You will keep up the communication with the horse's mouth with the taking and giving of the rein aids. The restraining rein aid is an extension of the restricting leg aid: it extends the imaginary side fence up the horse's head. The unyielding rein aid tells the horse that the communication with the horse's mouth is being interrupted, the motion of the fingers is stopped for a moment. Subsequently, however, the hand must release the movement again immediately.

The Full Halt

The full halt is used to bring the horse to a halt – irrespective of which pace it was moving in. Coming to a halt means that the entire motion is collected in one point, similar to catching a flying ball. Let us have a look at the process in slow motion: to begin with you determine the point at which you want to halt. Barbier suggests that the rider imagines a precipice at that point. Take a deep breath with the unconditional will to stop at that point. The legs form the frame on both sides of the horse. Breathe out and at the same time roll onto the rear ends of your seat bones. At the same time you catch the motion in the horse's mouth, hold the reins still for one or two chewing motions of the horse – no more! – and then let go of them again.

The more you get to the point of doing all these things simultaneously the more it will become clear to the horse what your intentions are. The correctly performed dressage halt is a lesson which requires extreme concentration, co-ordination in the seat and the communication with the horse. It is a movement of collection. Practise it once you have achieved a good co-ordination of movement with the horse and always use the minimum of aids. It is not important during practice that the horse comes to a halt in a closed position – with all four legs. What is important is that you develop trust in the physical communication and learn to talk quietly with your horse.

The Half-halt

The half-halt does not collect the motion into one point but instead attracts the attention of the horse with a "slight disturbance of the joint flow of movement". Let us have a look at this process in slow motion, as well. Instead of balancing your pelvis left – right, "cycling on your duck's feet", slip into neutral for a short moment, keep your "duck's feet" pulled back a little. Before the horse, however, has a chance to adapt itself to your change of motion and slows down (see exercises in the chapter "Communication with the Horse's Back – The Feeling for Motion"), push forward again. A light leg aid with the calf increases impulsion which is released forwards into the motion with the giving rein aid. And with that, you have smoothed over the slight action of disturbance, it does not become visible to the outside, and you continue to cycle with your "duck's feet" in the joint flow of movement.

The half-halt helps you to fine-tune the silent communication between horse and rider. With it you tell the horse something in the order of: "Please listen to me", or: "There is a dangerous rug hanging up front but the two of us will manage to get past it safely", or maybe: "I've got an idea – are you game?" You can also now say: "Come, we are going to canter now!", or simply just once in a while: "Hey, I'm here with you."

Can you feel the answer of your horse?

Imprint

Copyright of original edition © 2002 by Cadmos
This edition © 2002 by Cadmos Equestrian
Translated by Konstanze Allsopp
Design and composition: Ravenstein
Front cover and inside photos: Kristina Wedekind
Drawings: Esther von Hacht
Printed by Westermann, Zwickau
All rights reserved.
Copying or storage in electronic media is permitted only with prior written permission of the publisher.
Printed in Germany

ISBN 3-86127-933-9

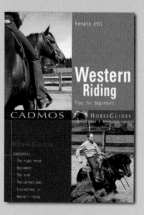

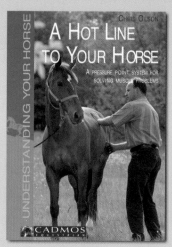